BLUEBERRIES LAVENDER

Songs of The Farmer's Children

BLUEBERRIES
LAVENDER

Songs of The Farmer's Children

POEMS BY NANCY DINGMAN WATSON

DRAWINGS BY ERIK BLEGVAD

ADDISON-WESLEY

Text Copyright © 1977 by Nancy Dingman Watson
Illustrations Copyright © 1977 by Erik Blegvad
All Rights Reserved
Addison-Wesley Publishing Company, Inc.
Reading, Massachusetts 01867
Printed in the United States of America
 BCDEFGHIJK-WZ-798

Library of Congress Cataloging in Publication Data

Watson, Nancy Dingman.
  Blueberries lavender.

  SUMMARY: A collection of poems exploring nature,
insects, animals, and childhood.

  [1. American poetry] I. Blegvad, Erik.
I. Title.
PZ8.3.W342Bl   811'.5'4   76-18226
ISBN 0-201-08568-2

CONTENTS

For Victor White
who believed when I was fifteen
and for some reason still does.

BLUEBERRIES LAVENDER

Blueberries lavender, blueberries blue
I will go berrying, Abbie, with you
We'll carry our sugar pails over our arms
And walk through the meadow past orchards and farms
Over the river bridge, orange with rust
Your soft little toe prints are warm in the dust

In Mr. Frost's pasture the blueberries grow
Blueberries high, huckleberries low
Berries of purple, inky and black
Crowding the trunk of the old tamarack
Berries of silvery lavender gloss
Hiding themselves in the feathery moss

Fingers are quick and my sugar pail fills
Till over the top the sweet purple spills
Now for my Abbie I'm off a-spying
Left in a mossy place, with fingers flying
And there on a stone with an empty pail
And purpley lips laughs sweet Abigail.

Then home through the meadow go Abbie and I
Home to our supper of blueberry pie.

BUTTERBALLS

Butter tastes so buttery, all golden like the sun
I like to be around when there is churning to be done.

Mother sets the milk pan on the kitchen shelf
I can skim the cream off and do it all myself.

The skim milk stays behind for the pigs to *slirrup* down
The cream goes in the butter churn for me to turn around.

It takes a lot of energy and when my arm goes *flap*
Mother takes the butter churn and puts it in her lap.

Her arm goes *churn, churn,* round and round,
    smooth as silk
And soon the golden butter comes and curds the
    blue-white milk.

She washes off the buttermilk and shapes the bars
    and calls
You've been such a help today, come get a butterball!

BLUEBERRY EYES

Blueberry eyes
As blue as the skies
Blueberry Thomas
Is picking for pies.

Blackberry
Thimbleberry
Fox grape pies
Purple as a prune plum
Blue as Tommy's eyes.

Cranberry
Gooseberry
Beach plum jam
What a good jelly-berry
Picker I am!

BARN CHORES

In the darkling early morning we go milk the Jersey cow
And jump in piles of sweet green hay, thrown from the
    fragrant mow

We feed the pigs and chickens and measure the
    horses' oats,
And cuddle the newborn kittens and play with the
    baby goats

We hunt for hidden nests of eggs and startle a
    deerfoot mouse
And crawl through dusty passageways to a secret
    haymow house

We sit in the antique sulky, and pull each other around
Like proper lords and ladies out for a day in town —

Then suddenly the farm bell rings, it sings
    a breakfast song
We hurry in and mother says, Children, what took
    so long?

SNOW

The strawberry hill is covered with snow
And blueberry bushes tick the ice
And windflowers lean on the drifts below
And the snow is trailed with the feet of mice.

I'm up on the hill, I'm deep in the woods,
I'm walking on wintery crust
And whenever I bump on a furry pine branch
I'm powdered with snowflake dust.

I stand very still and a crow *caw, caws*
A rabbit slips under a root
I hold my breath and the snow sifts down
And a chickadee hops on my boot.

CALICO BALL

O wrap yourself round in calico bright
Kathleen is off to the square dance tonight
Posters in the village advertise the great event
O swing your corner lady and do-si-do your gent!
She washed her party petticoat, polished her red slippers
Sewed on missing buttons and fixed balky zippers
Caught a pail of raindrops and shampooed her hair
And brushed it till it gleamed like a cat at the fair.

By four she had all her barn chores done
Had fed the baby animals one by one
Set the supper table, helped with the supper —
A dance is a wonderful speeder-upper!
Then O joy eight o'clock has come —
But Daddy's out milking and he hasn't got done!
Out to the barn she flies in a spin
To see if big Daddy needs help coming in.
Is Mother ready? I can hardly wait!
Come on Mom, come on Dad, we're going to be late!

The music has started, we're just in time
To get in this set. O isn't it fine
A plain quadrille and the right boy and girl!
See how my skirt goes out when I whirl?

O swing your corner lady and do-si-do your gent
The fiddler's still a-stomping and he hasn't paid
        the rent!

MY OWN ROOM

Up in my bedroom
On a winter's night
The fir tree ticks the window
When I put out the light

The sky is black and cold
The stars flash bright
The moon and clouds roll by
On the windy winter's night

I shiver as I watch
And I wish on a star
The first or the brightest
Or the one that blinks afar

And after I have wished
I jump into bed
And the fir tree ticks the window
All night by my head

But when a storm is raging
Or I hear an owl call
I like to know my brother
Is right down the hall.

SNOW WOMAN

Snow woman snow woman
What do you know?
You sit so still
And silent in the snow.

Snow woman snow woman
Do you like your hat?
You sit so quiet
And comfortable and fat.

Snow woman snow woman
Do you like your clothes?
Your apron and your mittens
And your big carrot nose?

Snow woman snow woman
Sitting in the night
Does the dark scare you
Or the cold moonlight?

Snow woman snow woman
Here comes the sun
Are you afraid of melting
And being all done?

SPOTTER AND SWATTER

Cammie takes the fly swatter
Caitie is the fly spotter
There's a fly! Wham!
Wham!
Missed him. Now he's in the jam.

SUGAR MAPLES

The snow in the sugar bush is up to my knees
But Peter says I can help tap the trees
So we harness up the horses and hitch up the sled
And shout *Giddy-up!* to big Tom and Ned.
When we reach the icy brook Peter lets the horses drink
But then we hurry over so the sled won't sink.

We're deep in the sugar bush and Peter hollers *Whoa!*
And the horses stand still in the quiet in the snow
Their nostrils blow steam and their coats foam white
And the birds stop to listen in the shafts of morning light.

Peter drills the holes and I stick in the spouts
And we hush and watch the first sweet sap drip out
I kneel beneath the spout and the sweet drips
    on my tongue
And then we tramp from tree to tree to get the
    buckets hung.

At noon we build a fire and eat a big lunch
And listen to the jaybirds scold and hear the
    horses munch
It's a long day's work, the big horses sweat
My mittens freeze stiff and my feet slosh wet
I'd really like to quit but I can't till we're through—
Peter wants to finish, and so I do too.

The sun is sliding down the sky — Let's head home!
    Peter shouts
The horses speed, the sled is light without the pails and
    spouts. . .
The kitchen's warm, and through the door there drifts
    amidst the clutter
The lovely smell of homemade bread and
    newly churned butter.

MY CAT

The man next door gave me a cat
There wasn't anything wrong in that
His wife told him he had too many
And *she* didn't think that I had any.

I didn't know what my mother would say
It depended a lot how she felt that day
And whether she might think the cat had diseases
Or would give my baby sister the baronical wheezes.

The man next door's wife baked a cake
And packed it in a basket for me to take
And they sent me off with the cake and the cat
And I couldn't see what was wrong with that.

The kitten really liked me and I felt so glad
To have a little kitten. But my mother was mad
She said to keep the cake so it wouldn't look rude
But the kitten didn't put her in a very good mood.

March right back, she said, with the cat.
Tell him thank you very much but we don't want that.
I said, I have an idea, let's keep the cat
And never mind the cake. We could send back that.

But then mother said, We won't discuss it any more.
And I took my cat back to the man next door.

MAKERS

Beetlebombs make jelly jam
And bumblebees make honey
Mommy makes the bread and cakes
And Easter eggs make bunnies

Bubbling springs make brooks and things
And rivers make the sea
Grownup frogs make pollywogs
But who made me?

PEEPERS IN THE SWAMP GRASS

Down in the meadow
Hidden from sight
Close by the crickets
Who creak in the night

Lives a little peeper
A green tree toad
He sings in the summer
When the grass is mowed

He sings in the swamp
Where the sweet spring drains
He peeps in the warm nights
And in the summer rains

Red-wing blackbirds
Whistle all the day
Beside the wet swamp grass
Where I go to play

But then in the evening
With darkness all about
The swamp fills with peepers
And the fireflies come out.

SPRING DIET

Nibble on a fiddle fern
Chew a birch twig
Sip upon a honeysuckle
Then you'll grow big.

ROOSTER RUE

Sing a song of rooster rue
Of flapping wings and cock-a-doodle-doo!
Morning is split with his lusty roar
King of the barnyard wakes once more
    Cock-a-doodle-doo!

Among the hens his red crest towers
Over their heads he glares and glowers
Looking for anything out-of-the-way
Get back in line there lady, he'll say
    Cock-a-doodle-doo!

Now from the henhouse with plumes unfurled
Swaggers the monarch, king of his world
While round about his harem gathers
And cluckingly answers his ruthers and rathers
    Cock-a-doodle-doo!

O you're a gorgeous handsome one
Your feathers scintillate in the sun
From peacock blue to turkey red
From plumed tail to hackled head
But you have grown so fierce and tall
Threatening egg-gatherers big and small
That you sing well of rooster rue —
Quite soon you'll be a rooster stew!
    Cock-a-doodle-doo!

FIRST ONE UP

Mornings before breakfast
Before the sun is up
When the moon sliver, pale and cool
Holds rain in a silver cup

I go to mother's garden
Where the honeysuckles grow
And grape vines hug the arbor
And tiger lilies blow

Birds warble from the woods
A bat swoops deep
Catching a last mosquito
Before it's time for sleep

Spider webs are bright with dew
The fresh-turned earth is brown
With molehills and daffodils
And dandelion down

And hollyhocks and mallow
And single pink roses
And on the ground like cold coiled snakes
The green garden hoses

I dream beside the daffodils
Their trumpets blowing sweet
Till the sun comes up and dries the dew
And I have to go in and eat.

GRASSHOPPER GREEN

Grasshopper green
Too quick to be seen
Jump like a Mexican jumpity bean!

Grasshopper high
Grasshopper low
Over my basket of berries you go!

Grasshopper low
Grasshopper high
Watch it or you will end up in a pie!

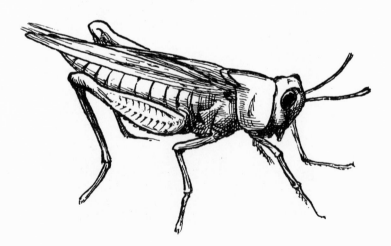

WALKING WITH THE GOATS

Through the hayseed meadows
Trip-trap trot the goats
Neatly clipping clover heads
Nibbling wild oats
Like pagan gods they gaze at me
With barred and amber eyes
Their pointed hoofs like dancing shoes
Disturb the dragonflies

The anxious doe pursues her kid
Bawling a mighty bray
Her bag flip-flops from side to side
And milk squirts on the hay
The infant Pan with budding horns
Bangs head-on with his brother
Until a pony shies at him
And drives him back to mother.

ZIZZY BEE

Down in the garden
Zooms the zizzy bee
And when I take a walk there
He zizzies after me.

Down in the orchard
The apple blossoms blow
And all the yellow zizzy bees
Make the apples grow.

Out in the meadow
I feel all alone
Along comes my zizzy bee
And follows me home.

Where does the zizzy bee
Go when he goes home?
I hope he has a mother there
And doesn't live alone.

BARN FIRE

Mr. Frost's barn
Caught fire in the night
And cows and horses bellowed
And screamed in the dark
And Daddy took me with him—he's a fire volunteer
The eerie siren rose and fell
And village dogs barked.

The road is very narrow
By the railroad bridge
It was lined with men and cars
And the tank truck was there
Trying to get water from the brook nearby
And all the while the horses screamed
And Mr. Frost cried.

He's a very old man
And he knows every cow
He wanted to get them out
And he *would* somehow
His friends held him back
While the fire hoses poured—
Sheets of water steamed and hissed
On the flaming beams and floor
I tried to help a little
But I got in the way
The hoses knocked me down
And the men said *Get away!*

Then they led the horses out
And the cows one by one
And they saved every animal
Before they were done
Mr. Frost was happy
It was bad about the barn
But he still had his cows
And his horses and his farm.

When I went home to bed
I couldn't get to sleep
I still saw the fire
And I worried about the sheep
And then Daddy told me
That the sheep had been outside
But I still got in his bed because
Mr. Frost cried.

YOU AND ME

Kittle kittle me
In a buttercup place
Strawberries, bluets and
Queen Anne's lace.

Chase me, chase me
Through the feather ferns
In the pink mallows
Where the autumn burns.

Push me, pull me
Rolling in the snow
Sliding down the hills
Where the windflowers blow.

Wish me want me
Where the maples bud
Slipper slopper after me
Sliding in the mud.

Green grass growing
Little calf lowing
Catch me, catch me
In a summer mowing.

MONKEY VINES

Down by the trickle brook
Through the green pines
Clyde and Linda take me swinging
On the monkey vines

I push out from the grassy edge
And kick my heels away
And when I reach the highest point
I think I'd like to stay

Suspended in the summer air
With sparrow hawks and crows
But then the vines swing back to earth
And pebbles scrape my toes.

A WALK FOR THINKING

It's quiet in the meadow
When we go for a walk
And mother doesn't hear me
Or answer when I talk.

She says it's a walk for thinking
Or to watch the summer sky
Or to look for ladyslippers
Or hear the wild geese cry

But I like to jabber
And tell her about things
Like sourgrass and bluebirds
And a fairy child with wings

And how the Johnny-jump-ups
Have faces and can see
I ask her where the moon is now
But she doesn't answer me.

But when we're walking home again
And evening shadows fall
I can put my hand in hers
And she hears me after all.

HIDING PLACE

Down among the cobwebs, at the roots of grass
Green and creepy quiet, dewy beads of glass
Little spiders spinning, beetles bumbling through
Ants in hurry-scurries, bustling on my shoe
Tiny flowers bending when the bees weigh them down
And bouncing up fluttering the butterflies around. . .
Down among the cobwebs and grasshopper spittle
I can hide and peek around and be glad I am little.

MOLEHILLS

I used to squash in molehills
Tramp tramp to the mole's door
But now I know it's a hall in his house
I don't do it any more.

HONEYBEE HILL

Here I sit on Honeybee Hill
Who can find me, I'm so still?

Watching birds in buttermilk skies,
Shivering from the goshawk's cries

Waiting for the whip-poor-will's call
Watching night's long shadows fall.

From the sugar bush warblers sing,
Loud a ruffed grouse drums his wing

Sunset paints in orange and pink
Ponds below where swallows drink.

If I sit here very still
On the grass of Honeybee Hill

From the woods might steal a deer
And *that* is why I'm waiting here.

UP IN THE PINE

I'm by myself
I want to be
I don't want anyone
Playing with me

I'm all alone
In the top of the pine
Daddy spanked me
And I don't feel fine

I can look way out
On the woods and lakes
I can hear the buzz
That the chain saw makes

And a woodpecker chopping
In the crabapple tree
With his red crest bobbing
But he doesn't see me

If anybody hollers
I'll pretend I'm not there
I may miss dinner
But I don't care

The pine needles swish
And the wind whistles free
And up in the pine
Is only me

It's starting to rain
But the tree keeps me dry
We toss in the black clouds
The tree and I

Now Daddy's calling.
He never *stays* mad.
He probably feels awful
Because I'm sad.

I'll answer Daddy.
He's concerned about the weather.
I'll climb down and he'll take my hand
And we'll go in the house together.

NOW

I ran down the steps
And out in the sun
I jumped in the air
I started to run
The dog got excited
She barked at a squirrel
We ran through the leaf piles
And set them a-whirl
The dust and the smokiness
Got in my nose
And tickled and sneezled me
Down to my toes
And just at that moment
I shouted out *Now*!
And the world seemed on fire . . .
I don't know how.

And when it's tomorrow
And oak leaves are dry
And trees are on fire
And flaming the sky
And Holly has left me
To follow a squirrel
I wonder if I will shout
Now! at the world?

Nancy Dingman Watson had a passion for education that moved her, as a child, to enroll in a candy-making correspondence course which "ended in mountains of fudge, cooked in the barn and bought by my Uncle Fred, who had a sweet tooth, up to a point. I tried taxidermy, too, but this was not a success — I forget why — and my father wrote a hot letter to the school of taxidermy and told them to stop sending me lessons. My cousin and I thought we might dig sassafras roots and make sarsaparilla to sell — nothing cliché like lemonade for me — but the stuff tasted like mud." She also wrote quite a lot, raised dogs, tried to raise canaries and rode her horse through cornfields and forests.

Since she's grown up, life has been different, but not very. She's written quite a few books, raised quite a few children, as well as goats, chickens, horses, organic gardens and bread doughs. Recently she's taken to beachcombing near the cabin where she sometimes writes.

Erik Blegvad was born in Copenhagen, Denmark, in 1923. He was a lazy child and studied only those subjects that interested him. By 1947 he had learned to speak English and German, to fly a light aircraft and to draw. Not all at once.

Now Mr. Blegvad spends his time illustrating children's books (over 75 titles), enjoying music (listening), drawings and paintings (looking) and bicycles (riding and tinkering with). He is married to an American artist who sometimes makes papier-mâché dishcloths and other handy household items. The Blegvads live in London during the winter and the south of France during the summer.